The Mean DAYS

Poetry by
Anne-Marie Cusac

TIA CHUCHA PRESS
Chicago and Los Angeles

Acknowledgments

I wish to thank the editors of the following journals for first publishing these poems, sometimes in a different version:

    Madison Review: "Miscarry," "Tinner"
    TriQuarterly: "The Necessity," "Poem for Jade"
    The Texas Observer: Part 3 of "The Mean Days," "The Life You Try Not to Think About"

I am indebted to the Stanford University Creative Writing Program for a Wallace Stegner Fellowship in Poetry. Those two years of support, camaraderie, and time were essential to the development of these poems. I am also grateful to the Wisconsin Arts Board for a 1997 Artist Fellowship Award, which enabled me to complete this book.

Many people gave these poems careful editorial attention. These are too numerous to name individually, but include my writing teachers at Northwestern University and the teachers and fellows at Stanford. Special thanks go out to those who helped edit the entire manuscript in its final stages: Rosemary Catacalos, Lisa Chipongian, Karen Fiser, Reg Gibbons, Cedar Marie, Meg Schoerke, Monica Serrano, and Ron Wallace. Thanks also to the staff at *The Progressive* magazine for continual support.

Finally, the longer poems in this book would not have been written without the innumerable hours I have spent in the kitchens, dining rooms, and backyards of my very large extended family. Unlike the stories I heard as a child, my narrative poems neither claim nor attempt to tell the factual truth—these are invented characters and stories. But the knack for talk among my relatives, in both the Midwestern United States and in the Maritime Provinces of Canada, has strongly influenced the form of these poems. For this gift, my extended family has my deepest gratitude.

Published by Tia Chucha Press / Luis Rodriguez, Founder and Editorial Director

ISBN 1-882688-27-9
Library of Congress: 01-132353

FOR INFORMATION WRITE TO:
Tia Chucha Press
The Guild Complex
1212 N. Ashland, Suite 211
Chicago IL 60622

Distributed by Northwestern University Press.
For orders, call 1 800 621 2736.

The Guild Complex publishes this book with the much appreciated financial support of the Richard H. Driehaus Foundation, the National Endowment for the Arts, the Illinois Arts Council, the John D. and Catherine T. MacArthur Foundation, the WPWR-TV Channel 50 Foundation, the Sara Lee Foundation, and other donors.

FOR THE TALKERS AND THE STORY-TELLERS

IN MEMORY OF
JADE CREIGHTON
LEO HARVEY
GLADYS CUSAC

Contents

Part 4: Ordinary Lies

Part 5: The Glass Box

Part 6: The Fresnel Lens

The Decision

Years later, the ease of it would come back to her
as she was scrubbing out the blackened pot
that wouldn't clean and wouldn't clean and wouldn't—
the way her mind, blundering into the corners
and dead-end hallways of her wedlock,
came to a door and touched it
and it swung out as if greased,
opening on a day of heavy sun.
Behind her lay the floor plan
of a decent life. Ahead was nothing
anyone had ever lived.

Part One

THE
MEAN
DAYS

The Mean Days

1 Family Picnic

That day, winds ran through the house, the tablecloths
wouldn't stay on. I slammed one window,
pinned a rug with a chair. I was waiting for Marly.
Then the porch boards sounded, the side door
rattling in its frame, and her voice:
"I'm going without you." Hurt
beat in my throat, I ran outside
so as not to let her win
what she had won.
Marly was scuffing up dust two blocks down.
She heard me in my best shoes,
stopped, and the wind broke loose.
Her words came to me
like the remains of words:
"There you are, sweetheart.
I must have forgotten you."

Together, we were mean. We didn't like women
trapped like parakeets in their dresses
and in their skins. We didn't like men,
solemnly proud of their whiskers
and taking up more space
than anybody should.
We liked ourselves,
we liked our husbands enough,
we had liked Hazel—but she was gone by then.

That picnic of dirty weather
the wind kept teasing our skirts.
Marly hollered with each puff,
"Bevvie, look there, look there."
We saw each other's
ordinary knees—
our thighs gone soft, our stockings
not quite fitting. Nothing remarkable,
but that day I liked us more,
except my niece, Pam,
who sat on her skirt
clasping her camera
until my cake
in a pre-tornado blast
lifted with its plate and flew
right at her mouth. Jimmy caught it.
Lovely story, really.
Her mouth stayed dry and lipsticked.
The color came off when she drank her milk.

Jimmy and Pam weighted all the platters
with rocks and condiment jars,
he as loose-boned as a pup,
she so tight and careful
it made me want to yell.
Yes, she'd have a piece
of that wild cake. (I wouldn't touch
something so unruly. I have enough trouble.)
Then she ate it
in little forkfuls

the way she must
at her kitchen table the size of a pond.
If you asked Jimmy and Pam, which I did,
they'd say they wanted
children. He'd say it.
She'd look at her lap.
But they raised retrievers
for sale, with a snarling bitch—
mostly males with big tummies.
Then gave them away.
They'd been doing this nine years.
That day I'd had enough of the way she ate.
I said, "Are you putting puppies in all those rooms?"

Marly said that was cruel,
but I don't apologize
ever. Something will come of my words.
Now Jimmy and Pam have a grown-up girl.
Marly, though, didn't come to my house
for eighteen days and evenings.
Then one morning she strides up the grass
to where I'm standing, knee-deep in bee balm,
bees at my skirt and gloves,
and plants a kiss on my mouth
and her lips stay there.
I see her eyes—
brown with yellow in the brown—
and my skull hums like the bees have gotten in.
After that, she was over every day
for coffee and milk, and never spoke of it.

Ten years ago, she started to stoop and her knee leaked,
then she died. Now I can't stop thinking
about the way things come to you and go
and you hardly notice.
I should add
we were married women, and happy.

2 What We Were Doing

Hazel was different. That fierce and gorgeous girl
had a brown velveteen coat.
You should have seen her—
elbows on the porch rail, her weight
making the boards click click as she
with a slow stare and a nod
watched the men
look back at her.
She was engaged
just enough times
not to go bad. I have a snapshot,
but it says little.
She was too much for the lens.

There's not a lot to Kickapoo Creek.
You can fish. You can wade
and pretend to swim.
I'd been married three months, Marly longer.
You could have wrung gallons from my hair.
We waded, we pretended to swim,

then, when Hazel pretended to drown,
Marly and I dragged her out of the water
in her close, wet dress,
her head back, her arms loose,
unbuttoned her,
pulled the dress off
(she came to life then),
undressed ourselves
and hung everything in the brambles.
Then a nap in the sun—
Hazel with her hair spread in the rocks,
arms crossed, her nipples tight, then relaxed;
Marly's long back, her hip thrust up,
hair in little tendrils at the nape.
The sun made me hot, the wind
gave me chills, the sun made
me hot again.

When we got home we
smelled like river.
Ben said, "What were you three doing?"

The next day, I helped Marly put in bulbs.
The clay got in my nails,
the kitchen tap didn't help.
I wasn't into fuss, but I liked clean hands
and kept scrubbing after Marly said
I might as well stop.
Speaking to her, I spoke into the sink,
scarcely above the water talking.

I said, "Marly, something's wrong with Hazel."
I said, "Marly, tell her to get married."
When I looked up, she bit a thread from her sleeve.

It took her more than a month to say it,
but Marly said she did, one afternoon
while Hazel stood in Uncle Matt's shed
hands on her hips and balancing
on one foot then the other
as she murmured back,
"Keep your voice down, all right?"
Later, at dusk in my yard,
Hazel ate a bowl of raspberries and asked for more.
She dripped on her front, but you could hardly tell.
The moon turned her dress blue-white.
She was a vivid girl,
a damn planet on my porch.
Marly and I, together on my stoop,
could hardly see each others' faces.
Hazel dropped a berry. It bounced off her shoe,
rolled, stopped. She flattened it with her toe.
Marly coughed, "You shouldn't
crush good food." Hazel said, "I do what I want."
Marly said, "You don't." Hazel said, "I do," frowned,
chose a berry, lifted it, didn't eat.

She married a broke cook from Decatur.
I saw her at the butcher's
where the Italian owner
liked me because I wasn't Italian

but was black-haired.
He gave me the sausages
his people fought over.
I took the lump of brown wrap,
turned to go, and found I couldn't breathe
because Hazel Harvey filled my head
with Hazel Harvey in her husband's coat,
her hair cut short, the cold heating her cheeks.
She said, "Hello Bevvie," pulled off her gloves
by tugging each separate finger,
then folded them both
into the pocket
of her husband's coat. "I'm pregnant."

3 She Stopped

They rented a yellow-brown house
with a yellow-brown yard.
Hazel put up curtains, swept, washed,
patched a gash in the wall, and
after three babies, stopped.
You hear about these things.
All afternoon, she sat away from the window
and told her little boy, Jimmy, give me the baby,
put the baby down, hand me the other baby,
and sent him out for beer three times a day—
morning, afternoon, night, even in snow.
Jimmy hated the trip, but he was a good kid
and Hazel needed it. Beer makes the milk come.

She sends Jimmy out for bottles. It's cold, he hesitates.
She flips the belt. The buckle knocks a chair. He remembers
but doesn't flinch. His eyes might flicker,
his head lowers, just that bit you
almost don't see; his torso doesn't move—
the way the dog guards her food.
Or she says, "Do the dishes." If he does them right
there won't be any problems, no problems.
Then, if there's enough light,
he can meet a friend down the bluff.
She's not up to the housework. She's worn out
with babies everywhere. But beer fortifies.

Ten years later, she left.
They dredged the ponds, they asked about a man.
There was no reason for it.
Just an absent woman
with four dresses in her closet.
For months, they held her shape,
her sour-salt smell, and another smell—of pine.

Jimmy helped me sort her things—
nothing worthwhile except her doeskin gloves,
which I took. Jimmy was a talker
who wanted life the way a boy of eighteen
wants to live. I sat in my chair and gazed
at her mouth speaking his voice, her eyes
restless, her hands working and working.
One day, though, he tells me, "Mom was so much
I think I've disappeared." So he gets married.

Tinner

It's not that way
with all things, some
that go are gone.

— A.R. AMMONS

Slung low on the water,
the river barges
lurk past the shut-down
coal towns, treeless dump heaps,
Mississippiward.

Forty-eight years
of metalwork, tinplate,
hardhead slag; and every
afternoon the river,
tin-colored, slipping from him.
Barge-tows docked for freight
only to leave. Nothing stays,
if it can help it, in Peoria.

He didn't.
In a year of strike, scab hirings,
the futile union and his body
breaking, he decided
to quit.
            One more grave, one more
suicide, and we
come to ourselves, a family

obliged to watch our own
failures repeat while, all the while:

        this is the river, glittering tin;

        this is the place he threw himself in;

        the Creve Coeur bridge. Remember.

Part TWO

NIGHT TRAIN

Night Train

She boards the car in a manner not quite fierce,
not a challenge, either, though one long-haired man
moves quickly from the doorway. Tall, her large
face emerging from the night outside,
she steadies two paper-handled shopping bags,
a bundled infant, and clasps the hand
of the young child who hesitates behind her,
clutching her dress, his face an unsaid "No!"
as she hoists him to the seat beside me; settles
the baby and herself across the aisle.
In the departing lurch she grabs a bottle,
begins to feed, and, in turn fed by
her infant's rhythmic and insistent swallowing;
his face, intent with pleasure, eyes half-closed;
or something else, perhaps the left hand
patting the bottleneck, or the right one
which opens slowly, slowly makes a fist;
she glances briefly, rarely across the aisle,
not seeing the other climb into my lap.
Until he has. She looks up, again looks down,
her eyes empty of anger or approval.
He smells of milk and talc and sits a moment,
his cornrowed head just below my chin,
then pulls himself to the glass, seeing the lights,
points at a distant building, pulls my hair,
and slaps his palm against the window, laughing
until he is tired and, suddenly, asleep.
I look up. Across the aisle his mother

sleeps too, still hugs the infant close to her,
nodding over it. I look back down—
his body slack and deeply, heavily warm,
face buried in my folded cardigan,
his breath unheard beneath the clatter, noise
of brakes, the nearby voices as we move
tonight, together, deep into the city.

Self-Haircut in the Port Authority

The bowler hat, fitted to his scalp
and set low, is his gauge
for the haircut
which requires such
conscientious rigor
it has gone on for hours.
His entire pale-brown bang
is now a strict
thumbs-width under the brim.
One hand locks on the scissors,
while his free index finger
touches behind his left ear
for the next piece, a centimeter too long,
which he can't quite find, then finds
and pulls, measures, pulls, remeasures
until he's certain
he's found it—
a strand the correct,
the perfect, perfect feel—
though he's not yet ready to snip.
All the while, his eyes follow
the female pigeon,
her rear cocked, her tail in a fan,
as she swerves and ruffles
and glances after the male
while he pecks at the dropped
and skidding button
he can't quite get.

Bus Depot Refrain

The angry child, her fist full of bread,
roars *bye!* at the next pair of headlights.
The more tolerant passengers wave, then wave again.
She doesn't notice.
The bus and her own face, unlikable in metal
and bawling back *goodbye!*, preoccupy her
until the bus backs off, shifts, goes.
Gone, she says in a hoarse voice to her bread, then eats.

The Life You Try Not to Think About

On the sidewalk, you don't stop moving.
You and the dog with three legs
that lunges away from handouts
but eats if the food drops
and the woman who keeps combing her hair
in hard strokes over the grate, and singing
in a furious voice,
He's dead, he's gone, lady, he's dead and gone.

But under the street, in the overhot depot
you can stay. Just keep yourself upright.
You can't sleep here. You can't do that. Get up.
Tonight, this submerged heat, lights no one turns off
and chairs the color of toast. The TVs cost.
Can I take your bag, miss? Never give up your bag.
Don't answer, don't look up. He is still here.

Arrivals arriving, departures departing.
The routes zigzag in a print that's hard to read
and means another town, this time the right one:
there it would be, the other life
you try not to think about,
except for the intimate voice
you can't place, which must come from there,
a strong one, low with a feminine rise, saying
You can't forecast the weather. No one does.
They're lying about that. They guess. And they guess wrong.
Then, with a drop in pitch, *He went and died*

and I'm tired. I'm so tired.
And something like *water* or *lost*
mixes with the sound of an engine turning over,
and you're still upright in an uncomfortable chair.
If you stay here, you can predict the next
push of bodies from the metal doors,
the reassuring ashtray scent, even the man
two seats away, who still wants your bag.

The possibilities gleam and stink in metal
and diesel. The losses
aren't worth counting.

But every ten minutes they shiver into gear.

Part Three

Three

SALT

MOTHER

Poem for Jade

Light gone out of day. In your small house
silence of button tins,
hot tea and oranges.

Outside, your son plays knee-deep in the ditch
and will not come, though you have called him in.
He disregards the snow
gusting the sky,
and how it shadows him and, deepening,
blanches and frets the new forsythia
until, in dusk, movement is snow.

A cancer of icicles
builds from the eaves.
You sit back, swallow twice. Your grey-flecked eyes
regard me. I
learn this again. Yes,
you are dying, the growth vigorous
from your lost breast into your bones.
Your gaze, brazenly alive.

And, when your daughter brings her doll,
porcelain, shattered from midriff down,
your finger, steady, traces a painted mouth,
a chin and brow, placid, expectant eyes.
Your daughter waits.
And you alone,
knowing you cannot fix what will not fix,
not knowing how to say that you cannot.

Salt Mother

I

The flats glint red and sun blares on the clay
as the river runs from the sea, bearing the smell
of something always, altogether lacked—
salt, raw, living. I can't help but want it.
A fist of clay, still wet, drenches the air.
Clay takes in sun. The touch is warm, a flesh,
though little grows on these flats but the river.

II

I've grown too old and she won't touch me, now,
except to plait my hair. She tugs it out,
frowns above me, parts it, and reparts it.

The place between her breasts smells of the river.
I don't tell her. I say the braids are tight.
If I swim, my hair soaks in the water.
All night I breathe the smell as if it's mine,
and dream, sometimes, the river is my mother
angered, who brims and runs unknowable.

Salt River

The halfwarm, red Peticodiac
drives at our wrists, and melts the skin of dust
to water flesh. I watch him through my hair.
Intent, he scowls toward the sun, crouches to wash,
and plunges his arm in—to the rolled cuff
again, again, the shattered river spilling.

I am no woman. I don't look right in the mirror,
but I'm here. I'm here. He walked so close to me
I felt the hairs of his arm. I've come with him
through pasture sunk in thistle, the hard sun
charging the yellow grasses. Since I must,
I follow him, rinse my burnt face, my neck,
taste salt and mineral. He watches me,
lies back, long, full in the sun, and watches.

The Sackville Twins

There are no photographs,
just two names: William, Walter.
The barn has gone and their boots
and tools, everything
except a story

in the old style—
mostly plot
and setting
and a refusal
to give motive—

a story we can't get rid of
by saying it in steady
voice upon voice.
I heard my Aunt
and my mother tell it.

I remember it the way I would
an intolerable light.

Look. They are walking
ninety years ago.
They lead a horse
across the Tantramar Marshes,
these two men, always together

.

even at night, in bed.
They are farmers. They never marry.
You can smell the sea,
the heat off their bodies
and the horse stink.

The animal stops,
stamps, starts again,
then mouths a flower
as Walter
hauls up her head.

No one knows the reason for
what happens next.
Walter starts running,
his hat loose, his hands out of his pockets.
He hasn't done

anything like this before
and William,
who doesn't understand,
pulls the horse's
muzzle against his chest.

Down the marsh is the barn.
For weeks, they've harvested salt hay.
The lofts are packed,
the air dust-loaded.
Walter goes in.

The building is grey, dry wood
until it bursts into flame.

William drops the reins,
leaves the horse,
runs. We are all
too late to this story, even William—
even the horse

that, minutes later, trots home.
In her yard, she snorts
and spooks.
The next afternoon, William
finds her eating flowers.

He recites this story once,
without tears, as an old man
to a nephew, who tells
his children, who
can't stop telling it.

The Old Way

It was a cure
for the baby's scream
that enters the brain
the way a worm does a pear.
Grip the ankles,
turn her upside-down,
give a shake.
It works almost instantly
and the sound from her
is like a dog trying to hold
a ball in its mouth and bark.
Turn her over again and see
her sweet pink baffled silent face.

Sometimes, the cure makes
a strange child
who doesn't sit up
or use her arms.
But no one knows for sure
how this one came to be.
Her language
has no meaning but music
from the forest
where a spring bubbles
through the floor
of a pond so cold
the children can't bear to wade in it.

The Most Beautiful Place

1

Her name is Louisa. She can't move.
Her mother wants
to care for her well, though her brain revolts
at this child so not quite a child.

Louisa grows
heavy, like any other daughter.

2

Her mother doesn't intend neglect
but for some reason there are days
she can't stop watching her own face on the window.

The sky changes color
as a clear place opens in her head.

3

Louisa has three sisters.
Today they run home from school on wool-covered legs
in a kind of ecstasy, with heat in their cheeks.

They package her in a blanket,

so her face peeks out, relaxed, uncurious.
They are going on a journey
and may never come back.

They push her across the street, into the woods
as gently as possible, buggy wheels jouncing.

4

At "the most beautiful place"

(the words they speak only to each other
in voices that keep and give away a secret)

there is a pond like an open eye.

If you look in, you can see
the entire world
and at the bottom

a spring fingers aside the sand.
It's work to get there.

The buggy lurches. Louisa
doesn't cry or show alarm
but stares at the air four inches from her face.

5

Around the iced-over pond,
the birches are hands incapable of gesture.

"Look, Louisa," the sisters say. "Look at that."

6

Fifty years later, each remembers
differently what she was trying,
and failed, to show.

One remembers her own disappointment
at the pond that had lived in her mind.

Coming back, the wool itched her wrists
and Louisa wouldn't
look where she pointed.

Another remembers the shadows
between the trees
more than the trees themselves
as the place went dark,
becoming the unformed space
Louisa always saw.

The eldest still grows anxious.
Her sisters don't want to go home

and she scarcely knows the route
in daylight.

She fingers a pencil in her pocket,
stares at Louisa, who doesn't shiver
but must be cold,
and asks herself, fifty years later,
what are we doing here?

The Necessity

Motionless, she watches from the stair,
her face too serious for her ten years.
From the front room below, as though far off,
she hears her father's hard, accusing words:
how had she left her in that chair all night,
in February, no blanket . . . couldn't she
remember last year, how ill that child had been?
And, as though embedded in the dark,
her mother's answer, that she was so tired,
couldn't he understand? she was just tired
carrying her up and down the stairs
and all the other children and no money,
never enough money for the nurse
she should have had—wouldn't he understand,
couldn't he see how weary she always was,
how tired? Her voice rises, weary as
the weariness she claims. The children—Walker
and the sisters—listen in their rooms
as the dreary fight, begun three days before,
goes on, and will go on.
                                    She climbs the steps,
each movement taking her further from their words,
closer to the room—which, from the hall,
she sees is open still, candlelit
and silent as she turns and shuts the door.

Near the far window, on the little bed,
the child, still wrapped in wool against the cold,

is dead since morning. In the candlelight
her skin is flushed as though still feverish,
hair burnished, arms and hands so frail
in the near dark, they are lost in a blanket fold.
As she has every evening for three years,
she speaks the name, "Louisa," quietly,
as if, this time, somehow, to call her back;
touches her arm, anticipating almost
the cold, peculiar skin; and as if she's needed,
curls beside her in between the sheets,
tenses a moment at the sudden smell,
strange and intimate, and holds the child—
knows that this is something she must do,
not knowing why, just the necessity
to stay here, close to her, until the smell
means nothing more than darkness might, until
she can breathe slowly, normally, again.

Miscarry

To glimpse herself in the mirror might have meaning,
she's not sure what. She won't turn on the light.
The faucet spits. She works the bitter soap
into her skin, wrists, abdomen, her throat;
and her breasts lift. She twists her dripping hair,
absorbed, methodical, alone, she won't
turn on the light. Here touch is different—
for once it asks for nothing.

                                    There were four,
hairless, mouthless, unbreathing, nameless, who
could call them children? She remembers, though,
each will, the dogged fastening to life,
even when she guessed that she would lose them,
and wished, dreading the wish, that her tight womb
would relax and give . . . the way, in the end, it gave.

She knows them now, lost things. She knows herself
contained in the black glass, containing absence.
And this—it must be instinct—all this washing.

Part Four

ORDINARY
LIES

Gladdie Flynn on the Dangers of Fire

There was the woman
whose skirt caught
when she had her back turned.
She looked around
and saw what
was happening
and she said "oops."
Just "oops,"
like a little
spill you could
mop up.

Songs from the Half Woman

In a mirror, my sudden self
smoothes its sleeve and strokes its chin,
and in this recognizes my half-self,
then half-ceases to grin.

*

On my split tongue the vowels bubble.
Each word I speak is half a world.
From the other hemisphere, my double
chatters like a mockingbird.

*

She whom I love is half nowhere
and when I love I have that knack
of loving the half that isn't there
to love me back.

Toward Home

The bus sits, grunting like a tin bullfrog,
and we board: two plumpish girls; a bearded man—
evidently blind—his black lab dog;

a man and wife, each gripping the other's hand,
their faces like two shrunken currant berries;
myself with my bookbag, bought secondhand,

and a paperback where everybody marries
just before the final page. Seven of us
bound north to three small towns, though little varies

between one and the next—the anonymous
roads, paved now and numbered, through every town.
The girls laugh, then no sound except the bus,

idling. I think of reading, but don't, like one
returning, one who counts each moment lost
until she's found the place she left, again.

I know that no child's innocence, once lost,
can be reclaimed by entering her house.
The bus moves—there's a scent of exhaust—

and I sense her presence as we near the house
she still owns; where, one winter day,
my mother pointed to a blue titmouse

and reached to touch my bare arm in a way
she seldom did. I did not understand
and could not, cannot, undo my jerk away,

nor change her eyes, intentionally bland,
the subtle, perfect, stiffening of her smile,
the casual withdrawal of her hand.

Identity

The name I come with is Cusac.
Few pronounce it right.
Its closest rhyme is music.
No, not Muzak—music.

The trace-your-roots mailings say
"only two hundred people
on the entire planet
have that name today.

Would you like to buy
for $35.95,
plus shipping costs, a book
that will tell you why?"

Dad buys and finds it lists
himself and Jim his brother,
his sister Reb, his father
(long dead), a cousin who's probably pissed

but says he's pleased as heck
when we give him a call.
Oh, and a B.C. gold mine
—but no relation. We checked.

Yet Reb heard a great uncle say,
"the Cusacs came from the Czar."
"Ivan the Terrible," says Reb.
But I think Anastasia's star

drew her to (of all places!)
Peoria, to give birth
without the benefit of anesthesia
to five blinking faces.

Four managed to survive
and sign up at the factory.
A guy at my dad's plant says he
once met a live

Cusac who came from Prague.
On the map, Prague is yellow
and near Yugoslavia, my favorite word.
That night I drop on my pillow

and Prague glows on my wall, with turrets
from the encyclopedia.
The next day at school, I parrot,
"We live near Yugoslavia,"

though I don't know what it means
to live there in 1976.
Still, it's something
to set fire to, like a wick tip

we've dug out of the wax.
Then Aunt Reb says a Cusac
came from Scotland in 1800—
so Cusac derives from Cusack.

One year Dad visits Houston
and meets a woman from home
who says a World Wide Web site says
our name comes from ancient Rome.

All that black, thick hair
on nearly every Cusac head
means conqueror's blood. Peoria, ha,
we're from Rome, instead.

Still, when we get together
and look at the faces—
sometimes fifty or more—
that share our name, the place is

Peoria, a company town.
We gossip about ourselves and fill
up on Bavarian salad, chicken, jars
of olives and midget pickles.
We'll take the renown
of the old, spoiled Roman will.

Just don't tell us what we see here
(Jess in a flush from being tickled,
the polished shoes, the table,
the baby dancing in his pajama feet,
Aunt Della, a flapper once, now hardly able
to brace herself upright,
Uncle Thump with his sweet
smile, and those who are already tight)

is everything we are.

Loss of Innocence in Downtown Peoria

I had a room on the fourth floor of the hotel down there.
It was a loud place—the sound of shoes
came every night with some purpose,
first distant, then right at my door
and maybe a pause but no knock,
then away down the hall and SLAM.
It made me desperate.
Here I was, a young guy, alone with these
terrible sounds up and down the hall.
SLAM, footsteps, SLAM, footsteps, SLAM.

It got so I would sit in the window—
a car horn was relief, the air fresh
if the wind came up off the river.
I'd smoke, eat a hardroll, and listen.

Then, one night, maybe my eye caught movement,
I glanced two floors down. Ordinarily, I didn't
look in windows. And most of the flats had curtains.
But she had pulled them open
and stood there—a woman
with scruffy black hair. I could see just enough
of the stiff shirt cloth, a gleam
along her nose, and her hands
moving in and out of the light.
The shirt slips and drops. There is a body,
one breast in yellow and the reddish nipple.

She is there maybe three minutes.
Then the curtains close. Who pulls them?
Not her. She wouldn't have done that.

The next night, her hair is in a tight knot.
This goes on for I don't know how many days.
I see her all morning and afternoon
and dig postholes until I taste dirt.
After dark, her hair is either up or down.

Then one night she lifts her eyes and looks
right at my room and me on the sill,
and there is no expression on her face.

Her building was a four-flat. It was easy.
When I rattled the knob, the door opened.
I had to make her *see* me.
But there were no curtains on the windows,
there was no woman,
the apartment was empty.

I breathed in once and out once and ran.
Twenty blocks later, I found a black-haired girl
who seemed to understand.
I took her back. I didn't look out the window.
I said, "Wash off your lipstick.
Let your hair down. Put it up again."
She listened and gave me a serious look,
then, with slow care and a rough towel,
scrubbed the color from her mouth.

Four Love Poems

1

Substantial, a root flesh
(no heady blooms)
fed on hidden water,
it learned the night,
the cold
aching with itself
and the slow probe
outward, mute, unhesitating
in all directions.

2

In Wisconsin, bat shadows
slip into themselves.
Dusks, I walk Mink River Road,
wingtips
just not flicking me. The stirred air
is touch I crave.

Daylight, full August
endures itself,
the sun gives, demands.

3

The eucalyptus, white-leafed to the sky,
rides the surge and plunge. Wind south, chill, true,
while the walls sigh and fill and sigh,
the curtains all shuddering and I
drink up absence like a presence. You.

4

The doves fret at the nest
all morning. Shudder of wings,
the eucalyptus shudders
and, after a pause, the voice,
the utterance and throb
and pulse, once more, of a sorrow
which is, and is not their sorrow.

.

Part Five

THE

GLASS

BOX

Night on a North Wisconsin Road

Ahead a light flashes,
then another from the black
and we reach the ambulance,
the three squad cars, a crowd
of people who stand talking
in pairs, not touching the car,
the bright, shattered windshield,
or the yearling that must
have jumped the rail.
                            As if shaped
in the darkest cherry wood,
the body seems only
too polished, placed there
with the legs curled under
as in the jump, the head thrown
back, neck just too arched.

In the pasture,
the other young horses bunch
together near the barbwire
staring, stupid, in the light.
One pushes forward,
nibbles at the woolen
shoulder of a lingering
farmhand. The touch, such a thing,
perhaps, is needed. But then—
though nothing moves, the farmhand

silent, both hands in pockets—
the yearling shies
away abruptly, wildly.
In the ambulance light
the wide colored muzzle patch
glows freakishly pink, then white.

The Plot

It is the fairy story, the one with the bitter apple
and the black-haired girl sleeping in a glass box.
He told it to his daughter from memory last year,
how there was rose in the cheeks, even in the coffin,
and the black lashes blinked and moisture came to the eyes
as she woke and breathed the scent of forest rain,
then married and lived with a long, grey dog
and the man who lifted the glass and kissed her mouth.
The tale has come to the father every morning
for the past week. He understands
the plot. The plot is not useless, the plot
has a momentum that guides the hand he uses to cut
the bread they will carry for lunch.
He's a loving man, he lives by kindness.
These are his kindnesses—
a sack of bread she could live on for several days
if she were lost in the woods,
the winter coat (thinking of damp
in layer on layer of leaves) he tugs
over her clothes, and the brown wool socks
as she starts to itch and whine.
It's a day of sweat, quivering black-eyed susans,
and a sticky, angry child as he, with aggravation,
grants her another kindness: "Dress
yourself." She does so, in a dun-colored blouse,
no socks. The plot is right, he thinks, but
there is something missing about the father, the one
who will guide his daughter in her school shoes

into the woods and help her lose her way.
Why is it that the tellers left out the father?
Something in the question makes him hurry,
and he combs her hair as she tries to shake him off.
Then, to complete the tale,
but also for her health, he chooses
the reddest apple he can find
from the twenty or so laid out for ripening.
It is still summer. The fruit is puny,
knobbed at the top. Still, it's an apple,
his last gift to her. He tucks it in with the bread.

There are no glass boxes he can think of
in northern Wisconsin, in 1920. It is cheapest
to nail up a coffin from pine boards.
There was, though, one grey dog—part wolf—
that bit its owner's face. It was strung on a fence,
the skull shot-shattered, the paws like shabby velvet.
The turkey vultures teetered over the body
and didn't scare because it didn't move.
Not much in this town looks like the fairy tale.
The daughter, for instance,
is six years old, willful and pleasure loving, with her father's chin
and a scarred forehead from a fall against the stove.
The stepmother has grey
shimmering hair. She never yells. Her voice
explains again and again inside his mind—
while he tucks his pant bottoms into his boots—
that she will not raise another

woman's child. The father, the other betrayer,
is himself. But he moves at a distance,
confined inside a story he can alter
only in motive and detail—the way the little girl's sleeves
are too long and her head drops to the side
as she asks loudly, "Where are we going?"

Rule, Age Nine

The game goes like this:
she traps ants
in a circle
of stacked pebbles
she dribbles with spit,
and watches them
try to get out.
Some make it. Others hit
the slippery rocks,
fall back, begin again
as if there's no such thing
as learning,
twenty-four times.
She counts.
Then, if an ant
still panics,
if the legs can't stop,
she crushes it with her thumb
and removes the corpse.
Twenty-four times.
That's the rule
she made up herself.

A game like this
has its own day and night.
Night is the tiny body
between her forefinger and thumb,

the pressure,
the hard outer shell,
its collapse.
Daybreak is benevolence—
the ant she
lifts on a twig
and lets go
because it is bigger
or smaller than the others
or more desperate
or lazy.

The Animal

The swallows hug the gusts west-east
east-west, skimming the wind:
their wings pouch, flick, and quicken.
A tern flaps north
and sand churns sand. The noise is the dry breathing
of the vast animal who dreams our beach
and dreams the rambling castle
already in decline, the moat
stocked with the bones of five alewives, picked clean.

Back of the castle, where the grey lake brims
with something far too huge for comfort,
you wade alone. The tide draws at your toes
as if with fingers, tugs you, and you go.

Wind snatches your hair, and when you dive
I've lost you for the count
of two waves shattering at the sand.
The lake spreads like an endless mouth
and the tern flaps up again.
The undertow comes lipping, lipping.

Then you emerge and grin, alive
and anything but resurrected, dripping.

Part Six

THE
FRESNEL
LENS

The Lighthouse Keeper's Wife

1 Career

I tried child care, college, and took a job
as a tour guide for the historical association
at a lighthouse with an original Fresnel lens.

It's Cream City brick on a rotting lime cliff.
Inside is a piano, blue onion china, four stoves.
(One in the parlor the keepers heated on Sunday.

Now I open that room on the hour.
It exhales the air and light of a refrigerator;
the tourists exhale and step forward.)

The table is always set. I dust the plates,
and think sometimes of cooking myself supper
and sitting in her chair. But I don't do it.

Upstairs is a rope bed the keepers tightened weekly.
She gave birth in it seven times to seven boys
who, as they grew moustaches, left, came back
to marry on the cliff, and left again.

Each evening the Fresnel lens circled five wicks
and bent and sent their fire
sixteen miles out to Thimbleberry Island.

The clockwork needed winding,
the lard in the oilhouse
had to be melted and dragged into the tower.

It was shared labor, done through the night.
Without it, the turning would stop,
the wicks would sputter out, the lens

and its thousand complicating prisms
would sit, a dead eye
in an iron cage.

As a young wife, she wrote to her father,
"In the morning, it is my habit

to walk to where the sumac divides on the bluff.
There, I look out at the shoal.
Once the sun is up

and I have made certain no ship is trapped,
I let myself sleep a good few hours."

If the keeper's wife was ever pretty, she stopped that.
Her rectangular face couldn't help its stare, her hair
thinned—there are photographs
that show her wide, imperfect part.

For water, she went hand over hand down a ladder—
in winter, if there was little snow, with a hatchet for ice.

2 The Hand

It started the night I took myself out to supper
for no reason, except I was thirty-seven
and alone and sick with the shadows of my apartment.

The tree in the yard has a limb that needs trimming.
On windy nights it taps at
my window with a lag between the knocks
like someone wanting in and biding her time.

Sometimes I go to the window
and watch a thin grey hand approach the glass
and touch it and pull back and touch it again.

3 Busser

The restaurant smelled of gravy.
The tables were already set. I sat
and ordered potatoes
with gravy and a biscuit.

My waitress gave a smile with each flick of her pencil
then, heels knocking, went back to the kitchen.
But I'd glimpsed in the space between her arm and torso

another woman with a red face, who wore
the same striped blouse as the others
but too tight in the shoulders. She was different.

People who say that mean, "She was so beautiful
I couldn't help my eyes." I mean she was older
and a busser.

Two tables down, she knelt on a chair.
Her hair sagged from its clip, dragging across the dishes.
Under my breath, I said, "That's not hygenic."

She stopped, glanced at the kitchen, then sat on her heels,
her hands in loose fists on her thighs.
My breath dried my mouth until she jerked up her head

and watched me watch as her loose hair
touched a coffee cup lip, and she palmed the tip,
rolled it up, buried it in her bra.

Then she came to my table, smelling
of face powder, gravy, what work does to a body.
With perfect enunciation and half a voice, she said, "I dare you."

I said, "I like a challenge." She watched with her mouth
puckered and smiling both, her tray edging the table,
as she moved her hip up and down with it, adjusting.

I left, but sat in my car, repeating
"I'd do it again. I'd do it over again,"
and remembered how the hostess

heard me out as she wrote on a paper towel
in large black letters, "Stealing."
The lights turned off in the restaurant,

all but one outside spot,
and the women gathered under it for a smoke—
the hostess in a black dress too good for her job,

my waitress wrapped in fake fur past her knees. The others
shivered in their blouses and letter jackets.
The busser didn't show. I waited—

what did I want?
To see what I had done. To watch her posture
and whether she met their eyes.

The women stood in a huddle, smoking quickly
and blowing into their hands to warm them up.
When I started my car, only the hostess looked over.

4 The Lazy Susan

Three nights after my visit to the restaurant,
I sat in my apartment sipping my water
and saw myself sitting and sipping.

It wasn't like looking in a mirror.
All of me rotated slowly—
a woman with a pilled sweater
bunched around her middle.

She placed
her drink on a coaster
and twisted faster
until her face

and her wide, imperfect part
were a bright smear on the air. But
(I could still make this out)

she picked up her glass
with the same
deliberate motion,
swallowed, put it down.

It was the clearest thought
I'd had in months
and the most disappointing. I said,

"Woman, stop drinking water
and take yourself out to supper."

This time, the place smelled like pancakes.
I looked around. I even stepped into the kitchen.
The only busser was a kid.

5 *Tea Party*

On Saturday—a week later,
I opened my windows though it was early winter,
and I heard the sound of feet in gravel,
in leaves, on concrete,
again in gravel.

The feet went around the building
four times, each a little louder
until they stamped up the porch
and the busser filled my screen

in a red, too-big coat
buttoned to her throat
and a red-yarn hat she'd crammed with hair.

It flopped from side to side.
She unbuckled her boots,
stood in her socks,
grabbed the strawberry tassel, lifted.

The hair came down like a wing.
I said, "You want some tea."

She sipped her drink with a spoon,
leaning from the chair edge
to take it in her mouth.

She didn't lift her hair
when she answered,
"It's okay, it's fine."

"Right," I said, "Do you want honey?"
I got up and went to the cupboard,
came back with the jar

and sat myself in a chair near her
while I rubbed
the stickiness on my palm.

This had an odd effect.
It made her push the strands from her mouth and say,
"The rest of those girls are in high school—

and the hostess is half my age."
Her voice sped up, slowed down, sped up.
"Then I got off and she said, 'Woman, you're fired.'

For days I tried to sleep, but I saw your eyes
watching me steal and hardly ever blinking.
Now I see them, they're still the same."

Her hand hovered around her teeth
fluttering when she laughed.
One was black under the enamel.

I thought, Oh god, she doesn't want me to sit here
and got up and sat in a chair to her right.
Her hair had the sheen of caramel.

I got a sensation in the mouth
like the first taste,
then, after a half hour,

I'd eaten too much.
She went on dipping her spoon,
sipping, dipping, sipping.

6 *The Rope*

She came the next Saturday and five Saturdays after.
She sat at my table. Two hours
to get through a cup of tea with scarcely a word.

I sat where I saw only hair like a drop off a cliff.
For some reason it made me angrier week by week—
the sheer, dirty-blonde fall of it. Then one day, with a sip,
I said, "Your hair needs fixing. I should do it."

She started, knocked out of her two-hour reverie
of tea and teaspoon, then looked at me with meaning.
She said, "It doesn't need fixing." "Yes, it does,
or you won't find yourself another job."

That made her push her cup with a *chink a chink*
and sit upright and flip her hair over the chair back.

I tugged it, combed it, braided it, smelled soap. We were
two women, with a rope of hair between us.

After what I'd done, I don't know why,
pinning it up, I hoped . . . for what?
I couldn't have told you then,

but it had to do with becoming someone
who hadn't seen a strange woman
steal a tip and turned her in and gotten her fired,

who didn't have the brutality I couldn't
quite look at directly,
like a lit Fresnel lens.

The hairdo was done. I handed her the mirror.
Her fingers, finding the sleek top of her head,
touched and straightened the twists and the many pins.

The style didn't become her. Even I saw that.
She looked and looked in the mirror
for somebody who should have been there.

Then she said, "Well, isn't that better,"
stood up, lifted her coat off the doorknob
and pulled the strawberry hat down on her head
hard so hairpins stuck out the back.

7 *The Lighthouse Keeper's Wife*

It's been three months. At night I sit and drink water
and if there's a wind, listen to the hand at the glass
as I remember with precision what never happened.

It goes like this:

I plait a ladder from her hair and climb down to the bay
in a winter of little snow, a hatchet for ice
slung on my back. It's a hard climb. I have skirts.

The busser stands at the top wearing a high collar,
her body braced, her hair terribly thick
and the color of new rope, or Cream City brick.

She's wound the braid on a tree. Even so
it drapes down the cliff.
At the moment I come from the bay

with ice chunks in my pail, the hatchet on my shoulder,
she jigs the ladder just out of reach
and lets it down and draws it up again—
as my hand flails, grabs for it, and fails—

in a joke about the ultimate betrayal
she finds hilarious, her laughter skimming the ice
while numbness creeps along my feet
and my arm grows heavier than my pail.

Even she turns frantic with cold,
looking once, and again, over her shoulder
toward the lighthouse with four stoves and blue onion china,

though she neither leaves the cliff edge
nor tosses me the ladder made from her hair.
It's bright afternoon, then dusk.

No one starts the clockwork
or heats the lard.
She's thirty feet above me. There's no moon.